Global Cities
TOKYO

Nicola Barber
Photographs by Rob Bowden

Evans

Published by
Evans Brothers Limited,
Part of the Evans Publishing Group,
2A Portman Mansions
Chiltern Street
London WIU 6NR

VISIT OUR WEBSITE
www.evansbooks.co.uk

First published 2006
© copyright Evans Brothers Limited

British Library Cataloguing in Publication Data
Barber, Nicola
Tokyo. - (Global cities)
1.Tokyo (Japan) - Juvenile literature
I.Title
952.1'3505

ISBN 0 237 53103 8
13-digit ISBN (from 1 January 2007) 9780237 53103 4

Design: Robert Walster, Big Blu Design
Maps and graphics by Martin Darlinson

All photographs are by Rob Bowden (EASI-Images) - except Corbis 15t

Series concept and project management EASI – Educational Resourcing
(info@easi-er.co.uk)

easi-er

Contents

Living in an urban world

Sometime in 2007 the world's population will, for the first time in history, become more urban than rural. An estimated 3.3 billion people will find themselves living in towns and cities, and for many the experience of urban living will be relatively new. For example, in China, the world's most populous country, the number of people living in urban areas increased from 196 million in 1980 to over 536 million by 2005.

The urban challenge...

This staggering rate of urbanisation (the process by which a country's population becomes concentrated into towns and cities), is being repeated across much of the world and presents a complex set of challenges for the 21st century. Many of these challenges are local, such as the provision of clean water for expanding urban populations, but others are global in scale. In 2003 an outbreak of the highly contagious SARS disease demonstrated this as it spread rapidly amongst the populations of well-connected cities across the globe. The pollution generated by urban areas is also a global concern, particularly as urban residents tend to create more than their rural counterparts. The city of Tokyo faces all these challenges.

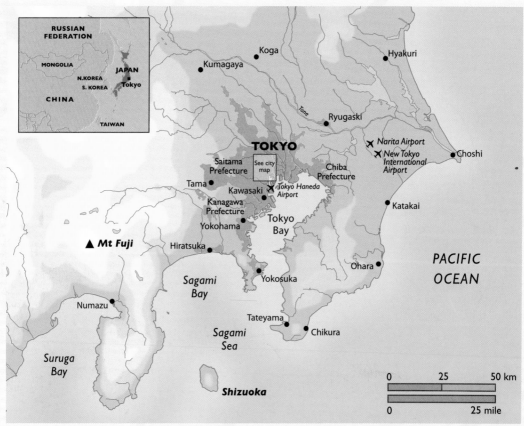

... and opportunity!

Urban centres and particularly major cities provide opportunities for improving life at both a local and a global scale. Cities allow for efficient forms of mass transport such as subway or light rail networks. Services such as waste collection, recycling, education and health can all function more efficiently in a city. Cities are centres of learning and often the birthplace of new ideas, from scientific and technical innovations to new ways of day-to-day living. Cities also provide a platform for the celebration of arts and culture and, as their populations become more multicultural, such celebrations are increasingly global in reach.

▼ An aerial view of Tokyo, the world's largest urban area.

A global city

Although all urban centres will share certain things in common there are a number of cities in which the challenges and opportunities facing an urban world are particularly condensed. These can be thought of as global cities, cities that in themselves provide a window on the wider world and reflect the challenges of urbanisation, of globalisation, of citizenship and of sustainable development, that face us all. Tokyo is one such city. It has been suffering from a protracted recession, yet it is one of the liveliest and most vibrant cities in the world. It is a concrete jungle, yet it includes mountains, ocean and rivers within its city boundaries. It celebrates its past throughout the year with traditional festivals and special days, yet it has some of the most exciting modern architecture anywhere in the world. Its skyline is a mass of cranes constructing expensive tower blocks and developments, yet it has an increasingly serious problem with homelessness. These are some of the contradictions that make Tokyo a global, and fascinating, city.

▼ Tokyo city centre.

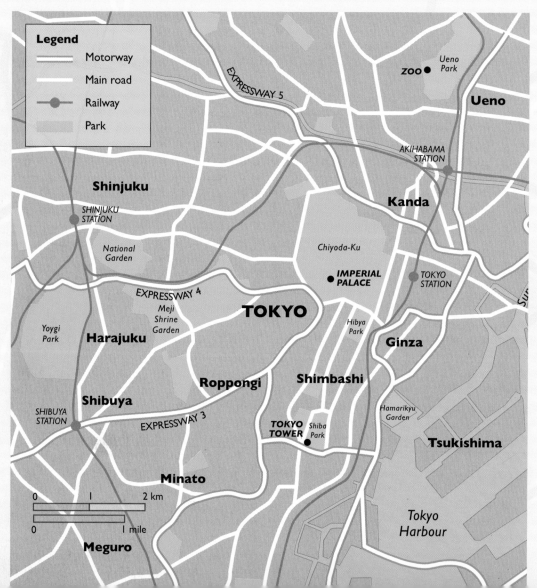

Legend

Motorway

Main road

Railway

Park

Defining the city

This book is concerned with Tokyo Metropolis (called 'Tokyo' throughout the book) which consists of a 'city' region, itself divided into 23 *ku* (wards), the Tama area to the west, and two island groups in the Pacific Ocean, the Izu and Ogasawara islands. The central 23-ward area covers 621 sq km, the larger Tama area 1,160 sq km and the islands have a total area of about 406 sq km. A much larger administrative area, known as the Greater Tokyo Area, includes the Metropolis described above as well as the three neighbouring *ken* (prefectures) of Chiba, Saitama and Kanagawa. This region contains around 26 per cent of the entire Japanese population – nearly 33 million people.

▼ The Asahi flame building designed by Philippe Starck, and (inset) the neon strip of Shinjuku, one of the main entertainment and shopping districts.

History of the city

Modern-day Tokyo is built on the site of an earlier city called Edo. In 1457, a warlord-poet by the name of Ota Dokan constructed fortifications in Edo, and it is he who is celebrated today as the city's original founder. But Edo remained a small village until the arrival of the warlord Tokugawa Ieyasu in 1590.

Tokugawa was given the title of *shogun* (military administrator) by the Kyoto-based emperor in 1603, and the Tokugawa shogunate was to rule Japan on behalf of the emperor until 1868. Tokugawa established his government in Edo and a time of rapid expansion followed. In order to control potential rivals, Tokugawa devised a system which obliged *daimyo* (feudal lords) to spend one year out of every two in Edo, away from their own lands, and to leave their wives and children in Edo at all times. Despite a terrible fire in 1657 which devastated much of the city and killed over 100,000 people, by the early 18th century, Edo's population stood at over one million – very large for the period.

▲ A model at the Edo Museum shows part of Tokyo as it would have appeared during the Edo period.

Isolation

In 1639, Ieyasu's grandson, Tokugawa Iemitsu, introduced the policy of 'sakoku', closing the country to foreign trade and influences. Japan's isolation continued until the arrival in Tokyo Bay of Commodore Matthew Perry's four 'black ships' in 1853. The purpose of this US expedition was to force Japan to open its ports to foreign trade and end its policy of *sakoku*. The turmoil that followed the opening of Japan led to the overthrow of the Tokugawa shoguns in 1868 and the restoration of power to Emperor Meiji. In 1868, the emperor moved the capital of Japan from Kyoto to Edo, renaming the city Tokyo (eastern capital).

Westernisation

The Meiji Period (1868-1912) saw the rapid Westernisation of Japan. Tokyo boomed as factories were built along the Sumida River, and Western-style buildings appeared in fashionable districts such as Ginza. Then, in 1923, disaster struck in the form of the Great Kanto Earthquake. The fires that followed the earthquake, caused by the charcoal and gas stoves in use across the city, destroyed much of Tokyo, killing more than 140,000 people. The rapid reconstruction of the city in the years that followed included the opening of the first subway line in 1927, and of Tokyo Airport in 1931. By the mid-1930s, Tokyo's population had reached over 6 million.

▲ The front of Tokyo station is one of the best surviving examples of Western-style architecture in the city.

▼ A guard house of the Imperial Palace was one of the only parts to survive air-raids during World War II.

World War II

During World War II, Tokyo and other Japanese cities became targets for heavy US bombing. In March 1945, a huge raid left large parts of Tokyo devastated and thousands dead. After the end of the war, in August 1945, Tokyo's population had shrunk to 3.49 million, half of its 1940 level, as residents fled the bombing for safer places outside the city. Massive rebuilding was needed to repair the shattered city.

Reconstruction

Japan was occupied by the Allies under the command of the US general Douglas MacArthur from 1945 until 1952. Japan lost its overseas territories, its armed forces were disbanded, and democratic government was set up, although the emperor remained on his throne as a figurehead. In 1949, Tokyo introduced the special system of administration which divides the city into 23 *ku* (wards) and which is still in use today. Ironically, the city's recovery was given a huge boost by another war – this time in Korea. Special contracts to supply the United Nations with weapons, tools and vehicles for the Korean War helped to kick-start Japanese industry once again. The construction of large office buildings in central Tokyo in the early 1950s offered visible evidence of the revival of the Japanese economy. People flocked to Tokyo to find work, and by 1962 the city's population was more than 10 million.

The 'bubble economy'

The rapid pace of development continued during the 1970s and '80s, interrupted briefly by the oil crisis in 1973 when the Arab-Israeli War caused the price of oil to rise sharply around the world. During the 1980s new wealth flooded into the city as the price of land and of stocks spiralled upwards, funding what became known as the 'bubble economy'. When the Tokyo stock market crashed in the early 1990s, the Japanese economy quickly went into recession.

The Olympic Games

Many people see 1964 as a turning-point for Japan: the year when Tokyo hosted the summer Olympic Games, and when Japan finally emerged from the shadow of World War II. There was a huge amount of building work for the Games, including the National Yoyogi Stadium in Shibuya which was designed by the Japanese architect Tange Kenzo. In the same year, the first *shinkansen*, bullet trains, began to operate between Tokyo and Osaka.

▲ The 1964 Olympic gymnastic stadium is still used today.

▲ The famous 'bullet train' connects Tokyo to the rest of Japan.

The 1990s

Other disasters hit hard during the 1990s. In January 1995, a massive earthquake (the Great Hanshin earthquake) devastated the coastal city of Kobe, killing more than 6,000 people and acting as a terrible reminder to the residents of Tokyo of the ever-present threat of earthquakes. In March of the same year, members of a cult group called Aum Shinrikyo released a nerve gas (sarin) on the Tokyo subway. The attacks killed 12 people and injured thousands.

In 1999, the people of Tokyo elected a right-wing, independent candidate called Shintaro Ishihara as governor. He was re-elected in 2003 and has attracted praise and controversy in equal measure during his term in office.

▲ Rescue workers after the 1995 sarin attacks.

▼ Tokyo has developed a strong retail sector.

The people of the city

With a population of over 12 million, Tokyo is home to 10 per cent of Japan's population. The city is the most densely populated area in Japan – 5,652 people live in every square kilometre. However, about two thirds (eight million) of Tokyo's population lives within the 23 *ku* (wards), with a density of 13,416 people per sq km. The remaining four million people live in the more spacious Tama area to the west. The Tokyo Metropolitan Government (TMG) is also responsible for about 27,000 people who inhabit the Izu and Ogasawara islands in the Pacific Ocean to the south of Tokyo Bay.

▲ Tokyo is one of the most crowded cities in the world.

▼ Most Tokyo residents live in apartments. Space is at a premium in such a crowded city.

Population trends

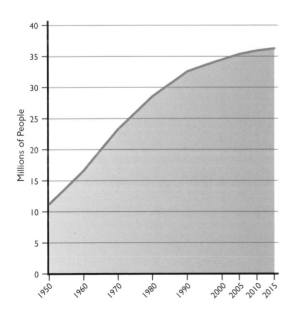

▲ In the *Tama* area housing is less dense, but residents may face a two-hour trip to work.

From the late 1960s until 1997, Tokyo experienced a decline in its population growth rate, as people moved out to the suburbs around the city. As the city's economy boomed, and the price of land in central Tokyo shot up, people found it impossible to afford the high prices of either buying or renting housing in the city. Many moved further out, either into the Tama area or into neighbouring prefectures, from where they commuted long distances to work every day.

However, since 1997 this pattern has begun to reverse, and people have started to move back once more into central Tokyo. This is largely a result of lower land prices due to the collapse of the 'bubble economy' in the 1990s. The demand for office space has slowed down as the economy has gone into recession, freeing up more land for residential use. As prices have fallen, some people have moved back into Tokyo to enjoy the benefits of city life, and particularly to reduce the time spent commuting (up to two hours each way for many workers). Attractive large-scale urban regeneration projects, such as the waterfront area facing Tokyo Bay or the Roppongi Hills complex, have played their part.

◀ The Greater Tokyo Area's population growth.

them. Couples in Tokyo who do have children receive financial help from the Metropolitan Government in the form of monthly payments and contributions towards childcare.

Ethnic minorities

Like the population of Japan as a whole, the people of Tokyo are mainly of Japanese descent. There are about 350,000 registered foreign residents (known locally as 'aliens') in Tokyo, including significant numbers of Chinese people (34 per cent), Koreans (29 per cent) and Filipinos (8.9 per cent). Many Koreans are descendants of labourers who were brought to Japan during the Japanese occupation of Korea, which ended in 1945. Today, many of the Koreans in Japan have taken Japanese nationality, but while some celebrate their Korean heritage, others still consider their Korean background a stigma which it is preferable to conceal.

Another group of people in Japanese society who try to keep their ancestry hidden is the *burakumin*. For many centuries, the *burakumin* did the jobs that were considered unclean – slaughtering animals or digging graves. Today, whilst any discrimination against a *buraku* is illegal, it is still widespread. There are about three million *burakumin* in Japan.

▲ As in the rest of Japan, Tokyo's population is ageing.

An ageing population

Two problems affecting the whole of Japan are the country's low birth rate and a rapidly ageing population. Surveys of Tokyo residents show that while nine per cent of the Tokyo population was over 65 years old in 1985, by 2003 this figure had almost doubled to 17 per cent. The percentage of elderly population for the whole of Japan reached 20 per cent in 2006, one of the highest figures for any country in the world. This trend will have a major impact on issues like health expenditure, and the Tokyo Metropolitan Government is already increasing its provision of homes for the elderly in the city.

The birth rate in Japan has dropped steadily since the 1970s, with an average of 1.2 babies for every Japanese woman aged 15-49 in 2003. Many women now have busy careers, and are choosing either not to have children at all, or are delaying having

▼ A Korean restaurant on the edge of Shinjuku, an area where many Koreans have settled.

Homelessness

Since the Japanese economy went into recession, homelessness has become an increasing – and increasingly visible – problem. The number of homeless people in Japan is estimated at 30,000, many of whom lost their homes after losing their jobs. In Tokyo, the homeless tend to congregate in makeshift camps in areas such as Ueno Park, despite the fact that pitching tents and lighting fires are illegal in the city's parks. While the park authorities mostly tolerate these communities, the government has often adopted a hard line towards the homeless. Tokyo's Shinjuku station once had a 'cardboard town' – rows of cardboard boxes used as shelter by homeless people – until a government crackdown saw the homeless evicted and the station 'cleaned up'. However, there are now several state-funded centres in Tokyo which provide the homeless with a bed, meals, and a base from which they can look for a job.

◀ The *Big Issue* magazine being sold by a homeless man in Ginza district. The magazine is published to benefit homeless people.

▼ Tokyo has a large population of homeless people.

19

Pressures of city life

Even for those residents of Tokyo who have jobs and homes, living in such an extremely crowded city brings its own strains and stresses – particularly the problems of intrusive noise and lack of privacy. Green spaces are increasingly seen as a vital resource in Tokyo (see page 54). Many Tokyoites use distractions such as *manga* comics (which originated in Tokyo) and playing *pachinko* (pin-ball machines) as forms of escape. Tokyo also has a very lively fashion and design scene which is an important aspect of life for many young people.

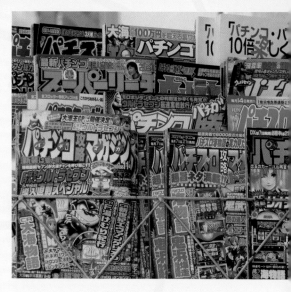

▲ *Manga* for sale. *Manga* are popular with all ages.

▼ Fashion allows young people to express themselves.

▲ *Pachinko* arcades offer a popular escape to businessmen.

A matter of faith

▲ Good fortune blocks at Yushima Seido, a shrine dedicated to the Chinese philosopher, Confucius.

'Shinto is for when you're born; Buddhism is for when you die.' This old Japanese saying sums up the attitude of many Japanese people to the two major religions of their country. While the rituals of Shintoism are part of daily life for many Japanese, people often turn to Buddhism for funerary and ancestral rites. There are many Shinto shrines and Buddhist temples in Tokyo, including Asakusa-jinja, a Shinto shrine which is located close behind Senso-ji, a Buddhist temple dedicated to Kannon, the goddess of mercy. The life of the city is also punctuated by both Shinto and Buddhist festivals (see page 47), many of which are public holidays.

▼ Meiji-jingu is one of the largest and most visited Shinto shrines in Tokyo, and is set in beautiful parkland.

Living in the city

Japanese children start school in the year of their sixth birthday, and attend primary school for six years, followed by junior high school for another three years. At the age of 15, compulsory schooling is at an end, but 96 per cent of pupils continue on to senior high school, for which their parents must pay. Those students who pass the intensely competitive examinations for a place at university then spend four years studying for a degree.

▲ Primary school pupils sit a test.

The education system

Most Japanese children attend some kind of pre-school before their official education begins, and, even from this early stage, many parents put great pressure on their children to succeed. Education is taken very seriously, and schools are expected to teach children not only the academic basics but also to provide moral guidance. In addition to their normal school day, many pupils also attend crammers ('juku') in the evenings and at weekends. However, in recent years this high-pressure atmosphere has led to increased problems with truancy, and with pupils 'dropping out' of the education system altogether. The recession has also had an effect on pupil morale: many students cannot see the point of studying for exams when they are unlikely to be able to find jobs at the end of their education.

More flexibility

The Japanese education system has been criticised for being too rigid, and concentrating too much on gaining qualifications. In response to these criticisms, the Tokyo Metropolitan Board of Education has drawn up various reforms which aim to promote individuality and creativity within the school environment. There is also a new emphasis on the importance of information technology, and of internationalisation – recognising that the future residents of Tokyo will be part not only of their local communities, but of a much wider, global community.

▼ As a reaction against their strict schooling these teenagers – *cos-play-zoku* – display fashion extremes.

Todai

There are over 100 universities and colleges in Tokyo, but by far the most prestigious is the University of Tokyo (Todai). All students must take a national test and a separate university examination for entry to a Japanese university, and competition is fierce. It is said that admission to Todai is a guarantee of lifetime success, as the university supplies the Japanese civil service and industry with highly qualified graduates. However, in recent years there have been attempts to reduce this bias by preventing graduates from revealing which university they have attended at job interviews.

◀ Students at Todai – the most prestigious university in Tokyo and Japan.

CASE STUDY

Yuka Fujimura (right) teaches at Kokusai High School in Meguru-ku, Tokyo. The school is a city school, and also a designated international school that accepts foreigners living in Tokyo. The school aims to foster in each student 'an understanding of, and respect for different countries, races, cultures and traditions'. There are students from at least 15 different nationalities.

According to Yuka, life as a teacher in Tokyo is generally good. Since the economic recession began in the early 1990s, teachers' pay has become better compared to other jobs. Teaching is attractive because it provides job stability during a time of economic uncertainty. Teachers are assigned posts by the TMG, but can stay only for a maximum of six years in one post. In particular, this policy was adopted because of the increasing numbers of children with learning difficulties reported in schools. Moving staff is a way to disperse specialist experience of working with such children throughout the system. Discipline is a growing issue, but varies from school to school. The average class size in Tokyo is 40 students, meaning that teachers are unable to give individual attention. However, at Kokusai, class sizes are much smaller – normally 20 or so – and so staff are able to devote more attention to each student.

Healthcare

Overall, healthcare in Japan is of a very high standard. It is compulsory to have private medical insurance, but this system is backed up by a government national health insurance scheme. The emphasis in Tokyo's health system is for patient-focused healthcare – trying to match the services provided with the changing needs of an increasingly ageing population. As in other countries in Asia, and across the world, globalisation has brought new challenges for Japan's healthcare professionals. Increased international travel between countries has meant that illnesses such as severe acute respiratory syndrome (SARS) have spread rapidly from country to country. In 2003, SARS spread from China (where it originated in 2002) to many other countries in Asia, including Japan, as well as Canada and the USA. In the following year, Japan was affected by avian flu, which had already ravaged other parts of Asia. Measures to prevent the spread of such diseases, and to deal with their effects, are a high priority for healthcare in the future.

▼ A street-side stall offering alternative remedies to the elderly at Kogn-ji temple in the Sugamo district.

A safe society?

Japan has a reputation as a very safe society in which to live, and crime levels are still amongst the lowest of the industrialised nations of the world. However, levels of crime have been increasing in recent years, and surveys show that Japanese people are increasingly fearful of crime and of the threat of terrorism. The rise in crime has been blamed on the recession and changing social trends, as well as on police corruption and outdated police methods. Controversially, Tokyo's governor Shintaro Ishihara has laid much of the blame for criminality in the city on juveniles and on 'undesirable foreigners'.

In August 2003, the TMG set up an Emergency Office for Public Security to combat crime in the city, with these two groups as their main targets. Juvenile crime is on the increase, and for many people the teenage motorbike gangs, known as *bosozoku*, that ride through the neighbourhoods of Tokyo are visible evidence of this fact. But the allegations against foreigners have been criticised by some people, who say that crimes committed by foreigners in Japan form only a tiny part of the overall crime statistics.

▼ Tokyo is a largely law-abiding city. These police officials are clamping down on illegal bicycle parking.

The *yakuza*

The *yakuza* are powerful criminal gangs that operate throughout Japan. These infamous organisations have their origins in the 17th century, and are still a powerful influence in modern-day Japan. Traditionally a *yakuza* had the top joint of one little finger cut off, and

tattoos covering much of his body, but this image is outdated today. However, although modern-day *yakuza* may blend in with the local population, they are still involved in illegal activities, and are reputed to have links with big business and top politicians.

Tokyo Alien Eye (TAE) was set up in 1999 as an organisation to help foreign students living and studying in Tokyo. It acts as a forum and information service, publishing information on the web and via email to alert registered users of housing and job opportunities. It has some 1,600 registered members.

Students coming to study in the city require accommodation and employment, yet a fear of foreigners (or outright racism) has led to enormous problems and forced many to abandon their studies. Many landlords refuse to rent to foreigners, and may even ask what 'colour' or nationality a person is over the phone. In Tokyo someone to act as a guarantor is required to rent a property, but finding a local (Japanese) guarantor is very difficult. TAE helps to find rooms for students and assists as a guarantor where possible. The same problems apply for foreign students looking for work, although recently McDonald's had been in touch with TAE to say that it was happy to recruit foreign students in Tokyo.

Most of this prejudice is against Koreans, Chinese, other Asians and Africans – Europeans and North Americans tend to have an easier time of things. All foreigners must carry alien ID at all times, and the municipal police have the legal power to stop, question and search 'aliens', while the foreigner living in Tokyo has virtually no rights. Foreign communities are forced to come to live together, creating mini-clusters such as the Koreans in Shikuan-dohri and Shinjuku. Even this is not a solution, however. There are, for example, Korean and Chinese schools in Tokyo that have been established to serve the Korean and Chinese communities, but the qualifications they produce are not recognised for university entry in Tokyo (those from British, French and German schools are!). Even if they get into university, 'alien' students find it very hard to get work once they have graduated.

Since the right-wing governor Shintaro Ishihara came to power in 1999, the situation has become worse. The police have been granted more powers and foreigners have become associated with crime through large amounts of media hype. All of this makes the work of TAE increasingly important.

Housing

Housing in Tokyo ranges from wooden, single-storey housing to high-rise apartment blocks. The two often exist side-by-side in central Tokyo, where there are few planning restrictions, and development has often been haphazard. The housing in the suburbs is mostly low-rise. However, whether a Tokyo resident lives in a city-centre condominium or a suburban house, he or she must live with the ever-present threat of earthquakes.

▶ Wooden houses can still be found in some parts of Tokyo, but are not common today.

The earthquake threat

Japan lies in the west Pacific earthquake zone, and is subject to frequent earthquakes. In 1995, a huge earthquake devastated the city of Kobe, about 400km west of Tokyo. The TMG has policies designed to prevent loss of life in the event of a major earthquake hitting Tokyo, particularly in relation to fire, which is the major risk following an earthquake. Closely packed, wooden houses have been one of the main causes of the spread of fire in previous disasters, so the TMG has implemented a programme to fireproof Tokyo's wooden housing in certain key districts. Open spaces such as parks and roads have an important role to play as refuges after an earthquake, and also act as firebreaks. To protect the city from the danger of flooding during and after an earthquake, river embankments are being strengthened and coastal defences improved.

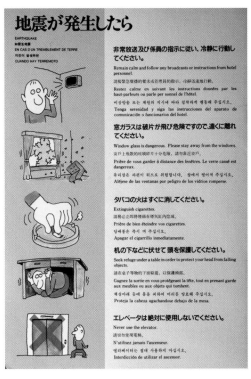

▲ An earthquake procedure poster in a Tokyo hotel.

▼ Works to strengthen the banks of the Sumida river.

CASE STUDY

The Kobe earthquake of 1995 was the first time a major earthquake hit a modern Japanese city, and many lessons have been learned from its aftermath. Although experts know that it is probable that a large earthquake will occur in the Tokyo area between now and the next 100 to 200 years, the difficulty is predicting exactly when. Given the problems of earthquake-prediction, the TMG has focused on its anti-earthquake measures to try to ensure that loss of life and damage can be restricted when disaster does, inevitably, strike. Staff at the Tokyo Metropolitan Disaster Prevention Center at the TMG headquarters in Shinjuku are on duty 24 hours a day, and emergency communications networks are in place to key locations such as the Tokyo Fire Department, the Police Department and hospitals. Seismographs, which measure the intensity of an earthquake, are situated all over Tokyo, allowing staff at the Disaster Prevention Center to collect immediate data, and to focus emergency aid on the areas that have been worst-hit.

Fire is one of the biggest hazards after an earthquake. The TMG has promoted the use of an earthquake-resistant petroleum heater which has an emergency cut-off switch. It also requests Tokyo residents to stabilise appliances in their homes such as boilers and stoves to try to prevent the outbreak of fire. Residents are encouraged to keep a store of water in the bath, or in a special triangular fire-extinguishing bucket, in order to extinguish fires before they take hold. The TMG even has an earthquake simulation vehicle which travels around the city, giving residents 'fire outbreak prevention training'.

▼ Part of the destroyed harbour in Kobe – a stark reminder of the permanent risk facing Tokyo.

Shopping

Even during a time of economic recession, shopping is a vital part of life for many Tokyo residents. Style and design are very important, and the multinational designer brands have a high profile in this fashion-conscious city where many young people have large amounts of disposable income. Shops range from the grand department stores such as Mitsukoshi and Isetan to quirky boutiques and small shops. The main shopping centres include Shinjuku and Shibuya, while Ginza is the most upmarket shopping destination in the city. Markets include the famous Tsukiji fish market, the biggest in the world, which is, however, due to be relocated by 2012.

▲ A trader at the 5.30am tuna auctions in Tsukiji fish market.

◀ Designer stores are clustered around the upmarket Ginza shopping district.

Tokyo through the seasons

For many Tokyo residents, one of the highlights of the year is *hanami* (cherry-blossom viewing). Some time around the end of March and beginning of April, Tokyo is transformed into a city of pink cherry blossom, and people celebrate the precious two weeks the blossom lasts with parties beneath the trees. Summers in the city are very hot and humid, and the streets hum with the sound of air-conditioning units. Late summer and early autumn can bring typhoons, but October and November are pleasant months, with cool, clear days. This is also the time of the year when the trees stun onlookers once again – this time with the reds, oranges and browns of their autumn foliage. Winters are cold, with clear skies and very occasional snowfalls.

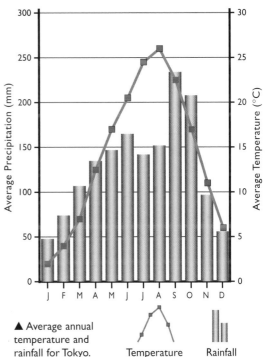

▲ Average annual temperature and rainfall for Tokyo.

Temperature   Rainfall

The city economy

The Japanese economy has been in recession since the early 1990s, when prices of stocks and land collapsed. Since then Tokyo, which had a reputation as an extremely expensive city, has become a less pricey place to live. However, about five per cent of the city's population is unemployed, and unemployment is especially prevalent among the under-30s.

▼ Most offices in Tokyo are designed as large, open-plan spaces.

Japan's trade

As Japan's economy developed during the 1960s and '70s, its main trading partner was the USA. The Japanese government implemented policies to encourage exports while at the same time strictly controlling imports into the country. The USA was prepared to tolerate this situation in return for having an Asian ally during the time of the Cold War. As the Japanese economy developed, it was controlled by powerful business groups, called *keiretsu*, who had close ties with government, the banks and each other. Employees who worked for these large groups were virtually guaranteed jobs for life.

In the early 1990s, with the Cold War at an end, Japan came under pressure from both the USA and the European Union to remove some of its restrictions on imports. At the same time, government regulation and the iron grip of large companies over the Japanese economy began to stifle innovation. Land prices had gone out of control, sent sky high by property speculation. This 'bubble economy' – so-called because it had grown like a bubble – burst as land prices and the stock market collapsed, and many banks and companies went bankrupt, with people losing work.

Employment today

The recession that followed has changed life for Tokyo residents. Many people can no longer rely on their companies for lifelong employment, and some have found themselves unable to find work. About five per cent of the Japanese population is unemployed, and in Tokyo many people under the age of 30 are unable to find full-time employment. However, retail prices, which had been artificially high in Japan thanks to the power of the big companies, have fallen, along with the price of land in the city (see page 17). Increasing numbers of women entered the workforce during the 'bubble economy', and women now make up about 40 per cent of the Japanese workforce. In Tokyo, about one fifth of the female workforce of around two and half million works in the retail and wholesale industries, with services, health and welfare and manufacturing also being important employers.

▲ Service at a department store, with six people to guide cars into the car park!

Tokyo's industries

The importance of manufacturing has declined in Tokyo since the early 1960s, as heavy industry and chemical plants were relocated out of the city. Manufacturing still plays a major role in the city's economy, however, with 22.5 per cent of the workforce employed in manufacturing and construction in 2000. Today, most of Tokyo's factories are small- or medium-sized enterprises, many concentrating on high-tech products and product development.

The vast majority of Tokyo's working population (74.2 per cent of the workforce) is employed in commerce, services or the transportation and communications industries. As many larger companies have been forced to restructure and scale down their operations as a result of the recession, people are having to be increasingly flexible in the job market. The TMG is trying to encourage the establishment of small- and medium-sized businesses in the city, particularly 'venture businesses' which concentrate on the research and development of new technologies. Many of these businesses are in the service and retail industries, others are software or Internet-related companies.

Commuters

Every day over two million people commute into Tokyo from outside the city. Even more startling, the census of 2000 showed that Tokyo's three central *ku* (wards), Chiyoda, Chuo and Minato, had a night-time population of 268,000 and a daytime population of 2.34 million! While this influx of people brings wealth to the city, it also puts a great strain on transport services and disaster planning and preparedness. The TMG is considering the introduction of a 'commuter tax' on people who come into the city from neighbouring prefectures, and road charging for road users.

▲ Commuters pour off the trains and into the city, a daily ritual for millions.

Tokyo – a financial leader of the world

Despite the problems of the recession, Tokyo is still one of the world's 'big three' financial centres (with London and New York), with the Tokyo Stock Exchange at its heart. Global brands such as Sony and Mitsubishi have their headquarters in Tokyo. However, a recent development is the rapid emergence of other global economies, particularly South Korea and China, as major forces. In 2004, China (including Hong Kong) replaced the USA as Japan's major trading partner. In addition, although many 'Japanese' products continue to be made using Japanese research and Japanese components, they are no longer actually manufactured in Japan. This is because many Japanese firms have moved their production lines to China to benefit from the much cheaper labour costs there.

▼ The Sony showroom in Ginza showcases the latest technology of one of Japan's leading companies. The products are often assembled in China.

CASE STUDY

The Tokyo Stock Exchange (TSE) was once a frantically busy place with some 2,000 traders shouting and gesticulating on its trading floor. Today, it is completely computerised, a process that took place over the 15 years up to 1999. Most of the traders, who worked for securities companies, returned to their company offices. The TSE's own staff number around 750. The building itself is now eerily quiet, with a huge glass cylinder on the former trading floor. Companies' stock prices are displayed around the top of the cylinder.

The TSE is a key global stock market and is very prestigious in Japan. Companies gain great credibility by being listed on the TSE. It sets the benchmarks and regulations for listing to take place, and then monitors trading and provides information to traders, individual investors and overseas markets. Every day, around 1.3 trillion Yen of trading (1US$= c.115 Yen) is monitored by the TSE. The TSE also manages the Tokyo Stock Price Index (TOPIX), which provides information about the performance of a wide range of Japanese stocks. TOPIX is considered to be a very accurate economic indicator and is therefore used by banks and by the government for their monitoring and planning of the economy. In this way, the TSE has an influence on the lives of people who are far removed from any of the actual trading themselves.

▲ The Tokyo Stock Exchange is at the heart of the city's financial industry.

▼ Katsuya Yamazaki is a manager at TSE, responsible for reporting irregularities in the market.

Urban regeneration

The opening of the 21st century has seen a construction boom in central Tokyo, with cranes towering over many parts of the city. These new developments are rejuvenating many areas of the city, and are backed by the TMG in the belief that such urban regeneration will help towards the revival of the Japanese economy. Some of the priority areas for redevelopment identified by the TMG include the district around Tokyo Station, the Tokyo waterfront area, the area around Shinjuku station, and a wide band that covers Shimbashi, Akasaka and Roppongi to the west of the Tokyo Bay area.

The New Marunouchi Building

Chiyoda ward forms the heart of the city, and contains the Imperial Palace as well as the business district of Marunouchi, an area that has sometimes been nicknamed 'Mitsubishi village' because of the large number of Mitsubishi headquarters located there. Because Marunouchi had such a high proportion of office buildings, it was bustling with office workers by day but relatively quiet at night.

Opposite Tokyo Station stood the old Marunouchi Building, owned by Mitsubishi and originally constructed in 1923, which had become a symbol for the whole district. However, Mitsubishi tore down the old building and, in 2002, a new building was opened in its place. The New Marunouchi Building contains not only offices, but also shops, restaurants and bars which have brought in new visitors, with the result that the area is busy not only during the day but also in the evenings and at weekends. The building has also attracted the University of Tokyo's Faculty of Economics, the Harvard Business School and the Stockholm School of Economics to move into offices there, opening up the prospects of closer links between these academic tenants and the many prestigious companies close at hand. It is this type of mixed-use development that the TMG hopes will help to kick-start the economy once again.

▶ The foyer area of the New Marunouchi Building, a leading example of urban regeneration in Tokyo.

▲ The food court in the basement of the New Marunouchi Building is just one of its facilities.

Smaller-scale projects

Another project shows what can be done on a much smaller scale. In another priority area for development, around Osaki station in Shinagawa ward, the TMG has targeted an area of land made available by the reduction in size of the local bus offices. The aim here is to create a mix of housing and shops, together with facilities that people need for everyday life, such as a daycare centre for children. Careful thought will be given to pedestrian access, for example to the local station, and there will be opportunities for small businesses.

Managing the city

Japan is divided into 47 self-governing regions called prefectures, and Tokyo Metropolis forms one of these prefectures. However, Tokyo is slightly different from the other prefectures in that it contains 26 *shi* (cities of 50,000 people or more) within its boundaries, and its central area is divided into 23 *ku* (wards), an administrative unit found only in Tokyo.

The Tokyo Metropolitan Government

The Tokyo Metropolis is governed by the Tokyo Metropolitan Government (TMG), which operates from its impressive offices in Shinjuku. The TMG is headed by the Governor, who is directly elected by the people of Tokyo every four years. Each of the 23 wards and the cities and towns in the Tama area also elect their own mayors. The TMG's decision-making body is the Tokyo Metropolitan Assembly, made up of 127 directly elected members who also serve a term of four years. The President of the Assembly is elected by its members.

The TMG has a close relationship with the 23 wards that make up the central area. In order to meet the needs of the densely packed population, the TMG manages services such as sewerage, water supplies and firefighting across all 23 wards. (In the Tama area, these services are run by the local governments of the towns and cities.) In order to fund these services, people in the 23-ward area pay specific taxes direct to the TMG. The TMG also oversees a system of financial adjustment which aims to ensure that there is a balanced distribution of financial resources between the 23 wards.

◀ The imposing design of the city government offices in Shinjuku. The towers are home to most government departments and have public viewing platforms too.

The national government

Tokyo is the seat of the national government of Japan. The Japanese Diet (parliament) building is in Chiyoda ward, surrounded by other government buildings. Nearby is the Imperial Palace, home to the Japanese royal family. However, in 1990, a resolution was passed in parliament to relocate the National Diet outside Tokyo because of concerns about congestion and shortage of affordable housing. The TMG is firmly opposed to such a plan, arguing that since the resolution was passed conditions in the capital have changed considerably – for example, land prices have dropped and the economy has gone into recession. While the economy of Japan is struggling, it makes little sense to spend the huge amounts necessary to move and rehouse the Diet and other government organisations. Furthermore, critics of the scheme point out that the political and economic centre of Japan lies at the centre of Tokyo, and that this concentration of know-how is vital to the well-being of the country and to its future recovery. The relocation plan is still under discussion.

▲ City-employed workers check traffic lights on a busy road into the city.

▼ The Diet (parliament) building in central Tokyo is the seat of the national government of Japan.

▲ A volunteer for a Japanese disaster relief group appeals for funds from passers-by.

The volunteer ethic

Tokyo's phenomenal economic success before the burst of the 'bubble economy' contributed to a society in which people worked hard and had little time for other concerns. The concept of volunteer or community work was alien to most people, but this has begun to change since the Kobe earthquake in 1995. More than 6,000 people died and hundreds of thousands were left homeless as a result of that earthquake. Thousands of Japanese people worked as volunteers in the aftermath, and since that time, volunteer organisations

have sprung up all over Japan. There is now a thriving volunteer scene in Tokyo, with people giving up their time to work with the homeless and the elderly. A new word, *vorubeito* – a mixture of 'volunteer' and 'arbeit' (the German word for 'work') – has entered the Japanese vocabulary. And while the focus of much voluntary work is on social welfare and community work, there is also a growing interest in global issues such as environmental matters, disaster relief and the relief of Third World debt.

CASE STUDY

The Tokyo Voluntary Action Center (TVAC) exists to help in voluntary action within the Tokyo area, but its activities also extend beyond to other parts of Japan and even to other countries. Since the Kobe earthquake many non-governmental organisations (NGOs) have sprung up, offering a range of volunteer activities. Nevertheless, volunteering is still not a key part of Tokyo society and is considered to be different and unusual. Many people live such high-pressure lives and have such limited spare time, that it can be difficult to recruit volunteers.

The TVAC is involved in citizenship education in Tokyo to try to encourage people to engage more as volunteers, or in whatever capacity they can, with their communities. One TVAC citizenship scheme is called 'Let's become an inventor for the community'. This scheme is run by TVAC together with the multinational General Electric and local schools. It asks General Electric employees to give up some of their time to be trained in citizenship and community issues. The employees are then teamed up with schools to have special days where they consider issues of importance to young people and help students to investigate these issues, think about solutions and then to develop community project proposals and presentations. The best projects are awarded with some funding, but it is more important that everyone gets involved and that bridges between young people, corporations and the local community are being built.

In 2003, the first year of the scheme, 129 General Electric employees applied to be involved, but as word has spread about the benefits of the scheme this number has risen dramatically, and in 2005 over 880 employees applied. This was too many for TVAC to manage, so some General Electric staff have become involved in training their peers – giving the whole scheme a greater degree of sustainability.

▼ A General Electric employee discussing local action with school children and their teacher.

Transport in the city

Tokyo has a good transport infrastructure which moves millions of people every day, but like most large cities around the world, it has major problems with traffic congestion on its roads. The number of people commuting into Tokyo from the prefectures that make up the Greater Tokyo Area (see page 32) put huge pressure on the transport system. For example, it is estimated that about two million people pass through Shinjuku Station, in the centre of the city, every day.

Airports

Tokyo has two major airports. Narita is the city's international airport and it lies 66 km east of Tokyo. Haneda is in the south of the city, and is the hub for domestic flights, handling 60 million passengers in 2002. As a result of the rising demand for internal flights, the TMG has plans to extend Haneda. The expansion is due to be completed by 2010, when the airport will be used for some international flights as well. The TMG is also putting pressure on the Japanese government to negotiate with the US government for the handover of a US air base at Yokota in the west of Tokyo. The TMG wants to use the airbase for private aircraft, to open up access to the west of Tokyo and help boost the economy of the Tama area.

▲ Tokyo Haneda airport handles hundreds of aeroplanes every day.

▼ Origin of commuters using the Tokyo transport network.

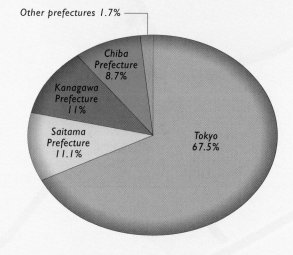

Other prefectures 1.7%

Chiba Prefecture 8.7%

Kanagawa Prefecture 11%

Saitama Prefecture 11.1%

Tokyo 67.5%

40

▲ The main container port in Tokyo Bay is one of Japan's most important trade connections.

Tokyo port

Tokyo is a major international port. It is a vital link in Japan's economy, as it acts as a distribution centre for exports and imports. Eighty per cent of the goods exported through Tokyo Port are manufactured in the Greater Tokyo Area, while 90 per cent of the goods imported through the port are consumed within the same area. In response to increased traffic in rival ports such as Hong Kong and Singapore, the TMG is planning to improve efficiency to speed up the transit time of cargo through the port, for example by the increased use of IT, and 24-hour working.

▼ A bullet train heads out of Tokyo.

Rail links

Railways link Tokyo with all other parts of the island of Honshu, while suburban rail networks connect Tokyo with its neighbouring prefectures in the Greater Tokyo Area. Japan pioneered the use of high-speed trains, known as 'bullet trains' *shinkansen*, in the 1960s. These trains run at speeds of up to 285 km per hour (177 mph), and link Tokyo with Japan's other main cities. The largest rail operator is Japan Railways, but a variety of companies run trains on Tokyo's extensive rail network. Combination tickets that allow passengers to ride on trains operated by any company, and in some cases on trains, subways and buses, have helped to make the transport system more efficient for users.

Subways and buses

The Tokyo Metro Company is in charge of eight subway lines in Tokyo, while the TMG runs four lines. Work on these lines is concentrating on making access easier and quicker for passengers, as well as trying to improve facilities for disabled users, for example by providing lifts between ground level and the platforms below. At the busiest times of day, in the morning and evening, people are employed to help cram commuters on to the subway trains, so great is the demand. Although there is an extensive system of buses, they are not as popular as the subways because they are subject to the problems of road congestion. Many buses are being made more environmentally friendly with the introduction of compressed natural gas (CNG) as fuel.

▼ ▶ The transport system, packed during rush hour, is easier to use out of peak hours.

▲ The main road routes in and out of Tokyo can become very congested at busy times.

Road travel

Traffic congestion is an acute problem in Tokyo. Data shows that the average speed of travel on the subway (33.5 km per hour) is faster than the average speed by car (26.1 km per hour). The rapid expansion of the city in the past meant that most roads extended radially out from central Tokyo, giving rise to a large amount of through-traffic in central Tokyo. The TMG is addressing this problem by the construction of various loop roads that will tie together these radial routes, and connect cities within the Greater Tokyo Area.

▲ There is plenty of provision for parking bicycles for those who use them.

Culture, leisure and tourism

Tokyo has an extremely vibrant cultural scene, ranging from the latest and hottest trends in fashion and design to more traditional Japanese pastimes such as *sumo* wrestling or *kabuki* theatre.

Traditional performing arts

The classical Japanese performing arts still play an important part in the cultural life of Tokyo. There are many different forms including *noh*, *kabuki*, *bunraku* and *rakugo*. *Noh* is an ancient form of dance-drama which can be seen in Tokyo at various venues, including the National Noh Theatre. *Bunraku* is puppet theatre, in which puppeteers manipulate large puppets while a narrator tells a story. The main venue in Tokyo for *bunraku* is the National Theatre. *Kabuki* is the grandest of all these traditional artforms, with spectacular costumes, song, dance and melodrama. There are several *kabuki* theatres in Tokyo, but the main place to see it is Kabuki-za in Ginza. *Rakugo* is comic monologue, Japanese-style, and takes place in several smaller theatres around the city.

▲ *Kabuki* acting uses dramatic costumes and gestures to emphasise the storyline.

The contemporary scene

Contemporary theatre and dance ranges from Japanese plays to productions of Shakespeare in translation, from hit musicals such as *Cats* to *butoh* – a modern dance that originated in Japan. The live music scene includes major acts at big venues such as the National Stadium, as well as jazz bars and live-music clubs. There are also many venues for the performance of classical music, including Tokyo Opera City in Shinjuku which opened in 1999.

▼ A local band perform an impromptu concert outside Shinjuku station.

CASE STUDY

Kabuki literally means 'song, dance and acting'. It originated in Kyoto at the beginning of the 17th century, and by the end of that century had assumed the form that is still performed today. All the roles in a *kabuki* play are taken by men, some of whom, known as *onnagata*, specialise in female roles. One of the most notable features of a *kabuki* theatre is the *hanamichi*, 'flower path', a raised walkway that extends through the audience to the back of the theatre and provides the opportunity for dramatic entrances and exits.

Kabuki is staged in seasons of 25 days. The same plays are performed for 25 days (matinée and evening performances are different) with a break of a few days before another 25-day cycle begins. The cast and theatre have only three days to rehearse new plays before going live! This is a very pressured system, especially as some actors may appear in both matinée and evening performances, with two completely different sets of make-up, costumes, words and movements to remember.

Kabuki is still very popular in Tokyo, and has become a favourite with tourists as well as locals, but in order to maintain its popularity, it is constantly innovating and trying to introduce new slants. For example, the plays presented are not always Japanese – plays such as those of William Shakespeare have been adapted for *kabuki*. The key is to adapt to the new era without losing the traditions of what *kabuki* represents – a difficult balance.

Kantaro Nakamura comes from a family that has been involved in this style of theatre since the Edo period. He is soon to become 'Kanzaburo' Nakamura, as he takes on the prestigious title of his father – the 18th generation son to take this name. His family were very influential in developing *kabuki* theatre, passing down styles of acting, ways of putting on make up and other traditions for hundreds of years.

▼ Kantaro Nakamura applying make-up before a performance.

many places that specialise in offbeat collections such as the drum museum in Asakusa or the kite museum in Nihonbashi. In recent years, a renewed interest in contemporary art and artists has been reflected in the opening of several new museums and galleries, for example the Mori Art Museum in Roppongi Hills, and Complex – a show-case for contemporary Japanese artists, also in Roppongi.

Tokyo has an amazing range of modern architecture, with notable contributions from the Japanese architect Tange Kenzo who designed the Tokyo Metropolitan Government offices in Shinjuku – the tallest structure in Tokyo. Other interesting buildings include the Asahi Flame, designed by French architect and designer Philippe Starck and topped by a giant golden flame, and the amazing glass hall of the Tokyo International Forum, designed by the US architect Raphael Vinoly.

Simple pleasures

It is only relatively recently that most private homes in Japan were equipped with bathrooms, making visits to the public bathhouses (sento) an important part of everyday life. Despite the fact that most residents in Tokyo now have access to private facilities, bathhouses are still found in Tokyo and are still popular. In such a crowded city, green public spaces are also important areas for recreation, and to escape the bustle of city life. At the heart of Tokyo lies the Imperial Palace (see page 13), surrounded by parks open to the public. There are other green spaces across Tokyo.

Art and architecture

The main centre for museums and galleries in Tokyo is in Ueno Park, which is home to the National Museum, the National Museum of Western Art and the Tokyo Metropolitan Museum of Art, among others. However, not all museums in Tokyo are on such a large scale, and there are

Festivals and fun

The year in Tokyo is punctuated by festivals (*matsuri*), many of which have their origins in Shintoism and Buddhism. Some of the most important include New Year, Adult's Day, Children's Day, Hana Matsuri (celebrating the birth of the Buddha) and *hanami* (cherry-blossom viewing). There are also annual cultural events such as the Tokyo Film Festival.

The most popular spectator sport in Tokyo is baseball, followed by sumo and soccer. Sumo is a sport that originated in Shinto rituals, and it dates back more than 2,000 years. Tournaments take place at the Ryogoku Kokugikan stadium, and attract large and enthusiastic crowds. Baseball was introduced to Japan in 1873, and Tokyo has various teams, including the Yomiuri Giants and the Yakult Swallows. Matches take place either at the Jingu

▲ A *mikoshi* (portable shrine) is paraded through the streets of Tokyo during Kanda Matsuri, one of the biggest annual festivals.

Baseball Stadium or the Tokyo Dome. Tokyo also has two J-league (Japan league) soccer teams, FC Tokyo and the Tokyo Verdies, both of which play their matches at the Tokyo Stadium.

▼ Sumo wrestlers compete in one of the three annual tournaments that take place in Tokyo each year.

Tourism issues

While 16.5 million Japanese people took holidays abroad in 2002, only 5.2 million tourists visited Japan the same year. The TMG is trying to promote the city as a tourist destination with 'The Tokyo Metropolitan Government Tourism Promotion Plan'. The plan aims to increase tourist numbers from 2.8 million in 1999 to a target of six million in 2006.

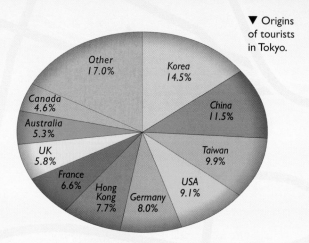

▼ Origins of tourists in Tokyo.

- Other 17.0%
- Korea 14.5%
- China 11.5%
- Taiwan 9.9%
- USA 9.1%
- Germany 8.0%
- Hong Kong 7.7%
- France 6.6%
- UK 5.8%
- Australia 5.3%
- Canada 4.6%

Providing information

The TMG has opened three Tourist Information Centres in the city, which provide information in Japanese, English, Chinese, Korean, Spanish, German and French. They give out advice about accommodation, travel and places to visit. In the past, language has been a major barrier for tourists, most of whom cannot speak Japanese or read *kanji* – the Japanese system of writing. In order to overcome this problem, increasing numbers of signs in the city are in both Japanese and English, particularly in areas that tourists might be expected to visit.

▲ Many signs in Tokyo are now bilingual as a way to promote more tourism.

▶ A man making and demonstrating traditional chopsticks at the tourist centre of the Metropolitan Government offices.

New ideas

The TMG has also gone abroad to promote Tokyo as a tourist destination. Sales teams from Tokyo have travelled to cities around the world to 'sell' the city to local travel agencies. In Tokyo itself, new schemes such as tickets that give admission to a variety of museums, and bus services between tourist attractions, have been introduced – all to make life easier for the tourist. Other new ideas include developing eco-tourism in the Izu and Ogasawara islands that are part of the TMG-administered area, and promoting the annual Tokyo Marathon as a potential tourist attraction.

CASE STUDY

Tourism was not really thought of as an industry in Tokyo until very recently. But when Shintaro Ishihara came to power in 1999, he considered it a key industry to help Tokyo rebuild and recover from recession. He set out a five-year plan that is now nearing its end, and in 2002 also formed a department for tourism. Major strategies included the establishment of information centres and bilingual signage, the opening up of cultural assets, and working closely with transport, hoteliers, local businesses and local governments – many of Tokyo's wards have their own tourism programmes. Discussions are now underway for the next phase.

Another strand in the promotion of Tokyo was to boost the image of the city overseas. TMG representatives have travelled to London in the UK, Berlin and Munich in Germany, and Los Angeles, New York and Houston in the USA to address businesses and agencies in the travel industry. The missions involved seminars and a market place for exhibitors to show off Tokyo's attractions.

▼ A multi-lingual worker at one of Tokyo's Tourist Information Centres.

The city environment

The TMG has highlighted urban warming as a major issue for Tokyo's environment in the future. Urban warming – an increase in average temperatures in the city – is partly a result of the global warming that is affecting temperatures worldwide. But it is also due to the very high concentration of concrete and tarmac across Tokyo, creating the so-called 'heat island' effect.

'Heat island'

Temperatures in Tokyo are regularly a few degrees higher than in the rural areas surrounding the city. In addition, average temperatures in the city have increased by 2.9°C in the last 100 years, compared to an average of just 1°C in smaller cities in Japan. The problem is that the concrete and tarmac of the city's buildings and roads absorb and retain heat. Cooling breezes from Tokyo Bay are increasingly being blocked by tall buildings, trapping the hot air in the city. Air-conditioning units, used to keep buildings cool, blow vast amounts of hot air out into the city's streets, and vehicle emissions also help to raise the temperature. The result is that the city swelters in the summer, with temperature soaring into the mid- and high-30°s Centigrade. Cases of heatstroke are rising, and there is an increased threat of diseases such as malaria and dengue fever becoming established as new types of mosquito thrive in the tropical climate. To monitor the 'heat island' phenomenon, the TMG has set up an observation network across Tokyo to record temperature and other data every 10 minutes of the day and night. It is known that vegetation helps to lower temperatures through the process of evaporation, so the preservation of green areas has become a high priority, and the TMG plans to increase the amount of green space per resident in the future (see page 54).

Rooftop gardens

Another 'greening' measure has been the introduction of roof gardens. A survey calculated that there were roughly 30 sq km of rooftops in Tokyo which could be converted into rooftop gardens, increasing the amount of vegetation in the city substantially. In 2001, a law was passed to require all new or reconstructed buildings on plots of 1,000 sq m or more to allot at least 20 per cent of their roof space to a garden. It is calculated that the heat released from a roof garden is just a quarter of that given off by a concrete roof.

▲ Workers crossing a roof garden during their break.

▲ A monorail linking central Tokyo to the redeveloped harbour area reduces the number of cars on the city roads.

Other measures

The TMG aims to reduce carbon dioxide emissions, and to promote reusable fuels. There are plans for district heating and cooling systems, using underground pipes to supply a whole cluster of buildings in a district with air conditioning, thereby saving energy and cutting down on the amount of pollution. In addition, many experts have called for a curb on the construction of tall buildings, particularly in the Tokyo Bay area, but although research is being carried out into the effects of skyscrapers and the 'heat island' phenomenon, with the new boom in construction in the city, this measure seems unlikely to succeed at present.

◀ An eco-friendly bicycle taxi in the Roppongi district of the city.

Tokyo's water supply

On average, the residents of Tokyo use six million cubic metres of water per day and the TMG calculates that it has water sources equivalent to 6.23 million cubic metres of water per day. Much of the city's water supply is taken from rivers, but as urbanisation has increased the quality of the water has decreased, requiring increasingly sophisticated purification processes before the water is safe for human consumption. As the demand for water rises, the need for new water resources will be met by the increased exploitation of the Tonegawa and Arakawa rivers, but the TMG is also promoting the idea that water is a valuable and limited resource, and encouraging people to take measures to save water wherever possible. While the whole of the 23-ward area is served by mains sewerage, there are still some areas in the Tama that do not have mains sewers. Many of the city's sewers and sewerage plants are over 50 years old, and therefore in need of upgrading. In the 23-ward area, a particular problem is that urbanisation has reduced the amount of unpaved ground through which rainwater can soak away. The increase in hard surfaces such as roads and pavements has led to a problem of 'runoff' – large amounts of water that cannot be absorbed and therefore pour into the drains, flooding the sewerage system. This can cause polluted floodwater to pour into rivers and the waters of Tokyo Bay. The TMG is addressing this problem by installing new pipelines and pumping stations, as well as reservoirs for the storage of sewerage during times of floods.

▼ A storm channel in Tokyo provides drainage for the heavy rainfall and run-off problems.

Waste management

Waste management is a major issue in Tokyo, particularly as most industrial waste is taken outside the prefecture for disposal. The TMG is concentrating on reducing the amount of waste that needs to be dealt with, and domestic recycling is strictly enforced, with separate collections for glass, paper, plastic and burnable waste.

▶ Refuse is carefully sorted into different types of waste for collection from dedicated points across the city.

▼ Waste is loaded onto barges for transport out of the city.

▲ A sign indicates a local waste collection schedule.

Green Tokyo

Green spaces are a vital resource for many reasons – recreational, environmental, and for more practical reasons (see below). However, the amount of park space in Tokyo is only 5.34 sq m per capita, far lower than in other international cities. The TMG wants to increase this figure to 12.9 sq m per capita in the 23-ward area and 21.9 sq m in the Tama area – roughly 20 per cent of the 23-ward area and 48 per cent of the Tama area. This is an ambitious plan, but the development of parks is seen as vital for the quality of life in the city. Parks also have other more practical functions in this earthquake-prone city. In the event of a major earthquake, each park will act as a vital refuge. Part of the TMG's plans include wide streets leading to the main parks, giving easy access in the event of such a disaster, and acting as firebreaks in the event of a fire. Increasing the amount of vegetation will also help with the problem

▲ Public parks are dotted across Tokyo, and provide green space amidst the the bustling city.

of runoff (see page 52) as more rainwater will be able to soak away, as well as with the problem of the 'heat island' effect (see page 50).

▼ A busy pathway in Ueno Park, one of the largest in the city. The park is also home to the city zoo and several museums.

CASE STUDY

In some schools in Tokyo, turf has been laid on school playgrounds to help address the problems of the 'heat island' phenomenon. Izumi Junior High School in Suginami-ku (above) was the first to undergo this schoolyard-greening programme. The grass was laid during 2002 and was funded and completed by the TMG, working with the local government. Six other schools in Tokyo have since undergone greening based on the success of this pilot school.

The green yard is managed by the community – not only parents and children who attend the school, but also members of the community in general. There is a maintenance committee that arranges for the grass to be cut every Saturday, and replaces any damaged or worn areas with plugs of grass cultivated for this purpose. Children are encouraged to get involved,

and every Tuesday the mowing club is entirely made up of children, because many other community members would be working. If the grass becomes worn then an area is cordoned off to allow it to recover. The grass clippings are composted.

Environmentally, the greening of a schoolyard makes a relatively small contribution to climate change and global warming – but it does have an impact. The high school next door still has a shale playground, and on a mid-summer's day the temperature difference between the two yards is as much as 10°C. Another big difference for the children is that they can play safely – instead of the hard and dusty gravel or shale surfaces of normal school yards, grass is relatively soft and fewer children are hurt when they fall.

The Tokyo of 2025

Tokyo is a constantly changing city, and one that has always evolved haphazardly rather than having any master plan imposed upon it. Its ability to adapt and reinvent itself will be the key to its future.

▶ Tokyo is still growing. This new building is part of the Tokyo Bay redevelopment.

▲ A couple look out from the Mori Tower in Roppongi at the ever-expanding city beyond.

Reforms for the future

Recovery from the recession is a high priority, as economic well-being holds the key for regeneration in Tokyo. The amount of construction in the city is an encouraging sign, and developments such as the New Marunouchi Building have been successful in creating fresh areas of excitement. Tourism, small businesses, high-tech research and development and contemporary art are all growth areas, as people have become less reliant on large companies and more entrepreneurial.

Planned reforms to education and welfare reflect the changing social situation in Tokyo. The education curriculum is being overhauled, with space allotted for subjects such as learning about Japanese traditions and for activities such as community service. The welfare service is opening more care homes for the elderly to make provision for Tokyo's increasingly ageing population.

Some of the most pressing reforms are to do with the environment, and the need to address the 'heat island' phenomenon. Disaster management is also always under review, with a high level of urgency given to flood protection measures along rivers and around Tokyo Bay to protect against possible *tsunamis* (tidal waves) after an earthquake.

◀ A meadow above an expressway through the city provides an example of how Tokyo is looking to become a greener city.

The Tokyo Megalopolis

Traditionally, the roads and railways in Tokyo have developed radially out from the centre, channelling commuters in and out of the city. More people are now moving into the centre of Tokyo, and a continuation of this trend may possibly bring with it a decrease in the amount of commuting.

In its future vision for the city, the TMG is promoting a different city model, the Tokyo Megalopolis based on a 'circular megalopolis structure'. The Tokyo Megalopolis would cover all the Greater Tokyo Area as well as the cities of Yokohama, Kawasaki and Chiba, and, with a population of 33 million people, it would be the largest in the world. The idea behind the concept is to reorganise the whole area into one huge circular structure, with loop roads and railways linking different zones, currently poorly linked, together. This would replace the emphasis on the 'city centre' and the 'suburbs' with one of different zones for different functions.

The TMG hopes that this plan would reduce levels of traffic, and therefore pollution, as well as alleviating commuter congestion. The plan extends until 2025, and its aim is 'the creation of Tokyo as a world-leading international city that is attractive and lively'.

▼ Young girls mix traditional and modern styles in expressing themselves through fashion. Their home, Tokyo, does much the same as it enters the 21st century.

Glossary

Bankrupt Describes a company which is unable to pay its debts. Can also apply to a person.

Big Issue A magazine originally founded in London that helps homeless people get a small income.

Bubble economy An economy that grows very rapidly and to unsustainable levels before collapsing.

Buddhism A religion that originated in India in the 6th century BC, that follows the teachings of the Buddha, the 'enlightened one'.

Bunraku Traditional Japanese puppet theatre using large puppets which are manipulated on stage by three puppeteers.

Butoh A modern dance form that originated in Japan in the 1950s which uses the human body to express extreme emotions.

Cold War The term used to describe the state of hostility between the Soviet Union and the United States that existed after World War II until the early 1990s.

Cos-play-zoku or the Costume Play Gangs are groups of mainly teenage girls who enjoy dressing outlandishly and posing in public.

Daimyo Feudal landlords during the time of the shoguns.

Diet The Japanese parliament.

Eco-tourism Tourism that takes account of both the environment and the needs of local people.

Hanami The festival of cherry-blossom viewing at the end of March/early April.

Heat-island effect The phenomenon whereby temperatures in a city are higher than in surrounding rural areas.

Infrastructure The basic structure of an organisation or a place, for example communications and transport.

Kabuki Traditional Japanese theatre in which all the roles are played by men.

Kanji Japanese characters, representing words.

Keiretsu Business groups with close links to government, the banks and each other.

Ku A city ward, an administrative area that is unique to Tokyo.

Manga Japanese comics.

Megalopolis A very large urban area made up of a series of conurbations that merge to form a continuous built-up area.

Noh Traditional ancient Japanese dance-drama, performed with masks.

Pachinko A Japanese form of pinball that is very popular.

Prefecture One of the 47 self-governing regions in Japan.

Radial Radiating from a central point, like the spokes on a bicycle wheel.

Rakugo Japanese comic monologue performed by one performer on a bare stage.

Recession A time of depression in economic activity.

Runoff Rainfall that runs away as surface water rather than being absorbed by the soil.

Sento A Japanese bath-house.

Shintoism An ancient Japanese religion in which followers worship many spirits (*kami*).

Shogun A military administrator before the Meiji Restoration in 1868.

Sumo An ancient Japanese sport which combines Shinto ritual with wrestling.

Tama The western part of the Tokyo Metropolis, outside the 23-ku area.

Typhoon A violent tropical storm.

Further information

Useful websites:

http://www.metro.tokyo.jp/ENGLISH/
The website for the Tokyo Metropolitan
Government.

http://www.jinjapan.org/
Japan Information Network for information
about Japan.

http://www.tourism.metro.tokyo.jp/english/
Tourist information about Tokyo.

http://www.bento.com/tokyofood.html
Everything you want to know about buying
food, cooking and eating out in Tokyo.

Books to read:

Countries of the World: Japan by Robert Case
(Evans, 2002)

Insight Guides Tokyo (APA Publications, 2000)

Lonely Planet Tokyo by Kara Knafelc (Lonely
Planet Publications, 2004)

*Underground: The Tokyo Gas Attack and the
Japanese Psyche* by Haruki Murakami
(Vintage, 2003)

Tokyo Style by Karin Goodwin (Chronicle
Books, 1999)

Manga
Tokyo Babylon (Tokyopop Press, 2004)

Tokyo Mew Mew by Mia Ikumi and Reiko
Yoshida (Tokyopop Press, 2004)

Novel
Tokyo by Graham Marks (Bloomsbury, 2006)

Index

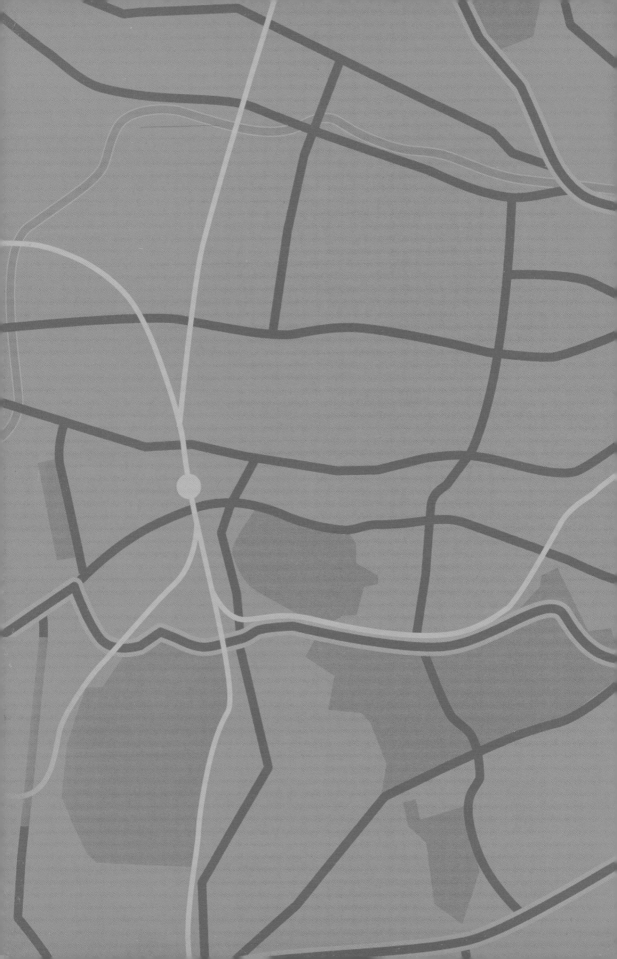